Simply Stitched with Wool

Simply Stitched with Wool
Published in 2023 by Zakka Workshop,
a division of World Book Media LLC

www.zakkaworkshop.com
134 Federal Street
Salem, MA 01970
info@zakkaworkshop.com

HIGUCHI YUMIKO WOOL SHISHU NO TANOSHIMI
All rights reserved. Copyright ©Yumiko Higuchi 2022

Original Japanese edition published by SHUFU TO SEIKATSU SHA CO., LTD
English translation and production rights arranged with Shufu To Seikatsusha Co., Ltd.
through Timo Associates, Inc., Tokyo and World Book Media, LLC, USA

Editor: Yumi Ishida
Book Design: Shoko Mikami (Vaa)
Photography: Shinsaku Kato
Contributing Photography: Boutique Jean Valet
    (P.6 linen dress, P9 jacket and skirt)
Styling: Kaori Maeda
Hair makeup: KOMAKI (nomadica)

Model: Julia Mahone (Sugar & Spice)
Instructions, Trace: Rika Tanaka
Review: Soryusha
Editor: Midori Yamaji
Translator: Kyoko Matthews
English Editor: Lindsay Fair

ISBN: 978-194055-281-1

Printed in China

10 9 8 7 6 5 4 3 2 1

Simply Stitched with Wool

Create Beautiful, Textured Embroidery with Wool & Cotton

YUMIKO HIGUCHI

Introduction

If you've never embroidered with wool thread before, you're in for a real treat!

Stitching with wool embroidery thread produces a beautiful, three-dimensional effect full of warmth, texture, and subtle variations in color. And because wool thread is voluminous, it allows you to stitch up bold, large-scale designs relatively quickly. Traditional cotton embroidery floss provides a lovely contrast to the wool, creating embroidery with a modern look and feel.

In this book, you will find a collection of both motifs and projects, all inspired by plants. I find the colors, shapes, and textures of plants very healing. Whether it's leaves gently swaying in the breeze or colorful flowers blooming, there is something so inspiring about stitching up these botanical designs.

Above all, my favorite thing about embroidery is the double dose of joy it provides. There is enjoyment both in the process of creating by hand and in the finished object itself—every time you wear an embroidered garment or see a sampler hanging on the wall, it will bring a smile to your face.

So grab your needle and thread and please embroider to your heart's content!

—Yumiko Higuchi

Contents

Wool Stitch Crest Motif

Instructions on page 46

This emblem combines a knitted pattern with a crown and pretty rose flowers.
Embroider this motif onto a square pouch, as shown on the opposite page.

Wool Stitch Crest Pouch

Instructions on page 47

Botanical Garden Sampler

Instructions on page 49

Colorful flowers bloom from spring to early summer.
This feeling of excitement is expressed in this garden sampler.

Mimosa Motif

Instructions on page 52

Sewn with French knots, these mimosa flowers are like bursts of spring sunshine. It's best to stitch the French knots last in order to avoid crushing them while you work.

Mimosa Shawl

Instructions on page 53

Flower Bed Motif

Instructions on page 54

There's something delightful about a row of flowers gently blowing in the breeze.
When stitching this motif, start with the stems and leaves, and add the flowers last.

Flower Rhythm Motif

Instructions on page 55

Worked in a simple color scheme, this repetitive floral pattern would be
lovely stitched along the hem of a skirt or the edge of curtains.

Butterflies Motif

Instructions on page 56

The wings of the butterflies are filled with wool thread. The black color scheme creates a sophisticated finish with a strong sense of presence.

Butterfly Beret

Instructions on page 57

Thistle Wreath Motif

Instructions on page 58

This luxurious wreath features plump thistle flowers. This motif can be used in various ways, such as the pot mat shown on the opposite page.

Thistle Wreath Pot Mat

Instructions on page 59

Vintage Flower Pattern

Instructions on page 60

This continuous pattern is created by combining voluminous flowers.
I selected low volume colors for this design to create a soft, calm impression.

Choose from three different designs inspired by blue and white Moroccan tiles.
I made them into pin cushions to use while doing needlework.

Botanical Garden Cushion

Instructions on page 64

Arrange a collection of blooming flowers onto a small cushion.
You can enjoy looking at flowers even when you're inside the house.

This sampler is bursting with poppies and other flowers. Use a similar shade
of green for all the leaves to really make the flowers stand out.

Dandelion Motif

Instructions on page 68

A dandelion is full of energy and appears as if its arms are open wide.
This symmetrical design is fun on its own or can be arranged in a group.

Modern Flower Motif

Instructions on page 69

Though the colors are gentle, this large flower creates a bold impression.
This motif will transform a simple knit sweater into a statement piece.

These flowers have a neat and tidy look. Sprinkle individual flowers across the surface of a tote bag to create a luxurious impression featuring chic colors.

Pressed Flowers Tote

Instructions on page 72

Bird Paradise Motif

Instructions on page 74

Bold red and blue flowers and lush greenery surround a playful bird and butterfly. This motif contains quite a few different stitches, so it's great for practicing your embroidery skills.

Funny Flower Pattern

Instructions on page 76

This small flower is cute and nostalgic, and a little quirky at the same time.
Enjoy selecting your color combinations.

Pansy Motif

Instructions on page 77

This bouquet of pansies features varying shades of purple, gray, and blue. Its simple shape is perfect for embellishing a small tote bag, as shown on the opposite page.

Pansy Tote

Instructions on page 78

Classical Flower Sampler

Instructions on page 79

Display this large flower design in an embroidery hoop for an antique feel. When stitching this type of flower, start from the center and work outward for best results.

Flower River Ribbon

Instructions on page 80

In this design, the ribbon represents a murmuring river and
vivid colors are used to express the flowing flowers.

Small Berries Motif

Instructions on page 81

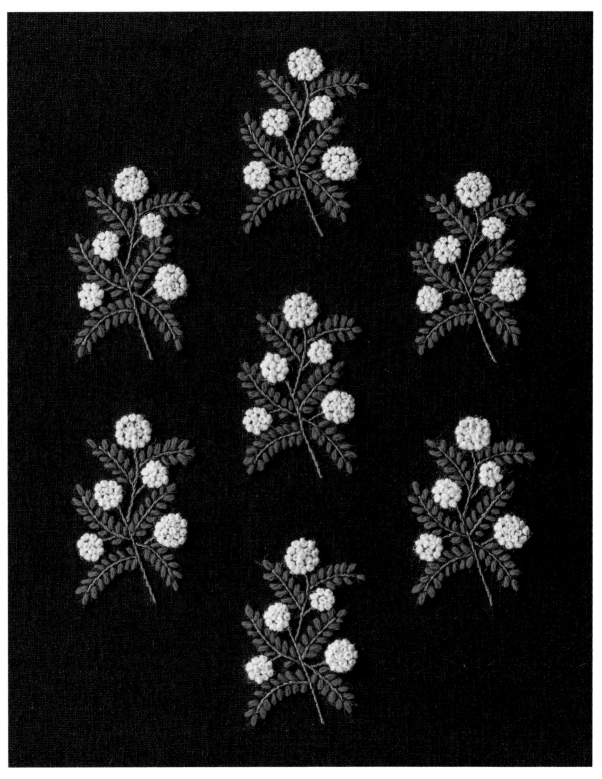

This shawl is decorated with three-dimensional berries. This motif is perfect for stitching onto garments you already own.

Small Berries Shawl

Instructions on page 81

Mushroom Sampler

Instructions on page 82

This seasonal design features mushrooms growing quietly in a forest.
A chic picture frame complements the embroidery.

Two skiers enjoy a snowy mountain. The evergreen botanicals
make this motif suitable for the winter season.

Christmas Rose Motif

Instructions on page 83

Though they may be rare, there are some beautiful, robust flowers that bloom
in winter. Use two different shades of thread for the leaves to add depth.

Christmas Square Botanical

Instructions on page 86

Enjoy seasonal Christmas flowers by arranging the motifs in a square to fit a piece of cloth or frame.

Materials

Thread

The projects in this book were made using three different types of thread:

a Appleton Crewel Wool

This wool thread possesses a thickness similar to six strands of embroidery floss, but it cannot be separated. It is available in lots of shades of beautiful, soft colors and is easy to work with, even if you are new to stitching with wool. When working with this type of thread, cut pieces about 24" (60 cm) long and use one or two strands.

b DMC Tapestry Wool

This thick thread has a yarn-like texture and cannot be separated. It is available in several different shades of vibrant, matte colors and produces a beautiful three-dimensional effect full of texture. When working with this type of thread, cut pieces about 24" (60 cm) long and use on or two strands. You will need a tapestry needle when stitching with this thread.

c DMC Six Strand Embroidery Floss

Also called No. 25 embroidery floss, this is the most popular type of floss among embroidery artists. It is composed of six thin strands of cotton that are twisted together. When working with this type of floss, cut pieces about 24" (60 cm) long. Gently separate the required number of strands, before aligning them and threading the needle. This will prevent the floss from tangling as you stitch.

Fabric

Linen fabric was used for the projects in this book. Soft, flatweave linen fabric works well with both wool and cotton thread. If you're new to embroidery, opt for a light or bright colored fabric so it will be easy to trace the design and see your stitches as you work. Linen may shrink the first time it is washed, so be sure to rinse your fabric before embroidering. Soak the linen in lukewarm water for several hours or overnight, lightly squeeze the water out, and let it dry in the shade. When the fabric is half dry, gently iron it to adjust the fabric grain as necessary.

Embroidery Care

Cleaning: If cleaning is necessary, take care to dry clean projects embroidered with wool thread.

Ironing: When you're finished embroidering, use a wet cloth to remove any stray chalk marks. Next, place a thick towel on your ironing board and align the work with the embroidered side facing down. Gently spray the work with water and iron with low heat. Pull the fabric taut as you iron to remove wrinkles.

a

b

c

Tools

a Needles

Use a tapestry needle when stitching with tapestry wool and a French embroidery needle when stitching with crewel wool or six strand embroidery floss. Refer to the chart on the right to select the appropriate size needle based on the number of strands used.

b Needle Threaders

Needle threaders are helpful, especially when working with wool thread.

c Thread Snips & Fabric Shears

Use a small, sharp pair of scissors for clipping embroidery thread. Use a large, sharp pair of scissors for cutting fabric.

d Embroidery hoops

Use embroidery hoops to hold the fabric taut while stitching. Use a hoop that is at least 4" (10 cm) in diameter or larger to stitch the designs in this book. Wrap a thin piece of bias cut fabric around the inner hoop to help prevent your fabric from moving and creasing. Tighten the screw as necessary to keep the fabric in place as you stitch.

e Pin Cushion & Pins

You'll need pins to secure carbon chalk paper to the fabric when transferring embroidery designs or to hold pieces of fabric together when sewing. Use a pin cushion to safely store pins.

f Carbon Chalk Paper

This paper is designed for transferring embroidery motifs onto fabric. Refer to page 45 for instructions on how to use this paper. You'll want to use white chalk paper when embroidering onto dark colored fabric.

Thread Type	No. of Strands	Needle Used (in this book)
DMC Tapestry Wool	1–2	DMC tapestry needle size 18
Appleton Crewel Wool	1–2	Clover French embroidery needle size 3
DMC Six Strand Embroidery Floss	1–2	Clover French embroidery needle size 7
	3–4	Clover French embroidery needle size 5
	6	Clover French embroidery needle size 3

g Tracing Paper & Cellophane

Use thin transparent tracing paper to copy the embroidery designs from the book. Layer cellophane on top of the tracing paper to prevent it from ripping when transferring the embroidery design. Refer to page 45 for instructions on how to use tracing paper and cellophane in conjunction with carbon chalk paper.

h Tracer

Use this tool to transfer the embroidery design onto the fabric (refer to page 45). You can also use an empty ballpoint pen.

i Water Soluble Stabilizer

Use this sheer, non-woven stabilizer on fabrics or materials that make it difficult to transfer embroidery designs using carbon chalk paper, such as dark colored fabrics, thick fabrics, knits, and felt. There is even adhesive-style water soluble stabilizer available that sticks to fabric. Refer to page 45 for instructions on using water soluble stabilizer.

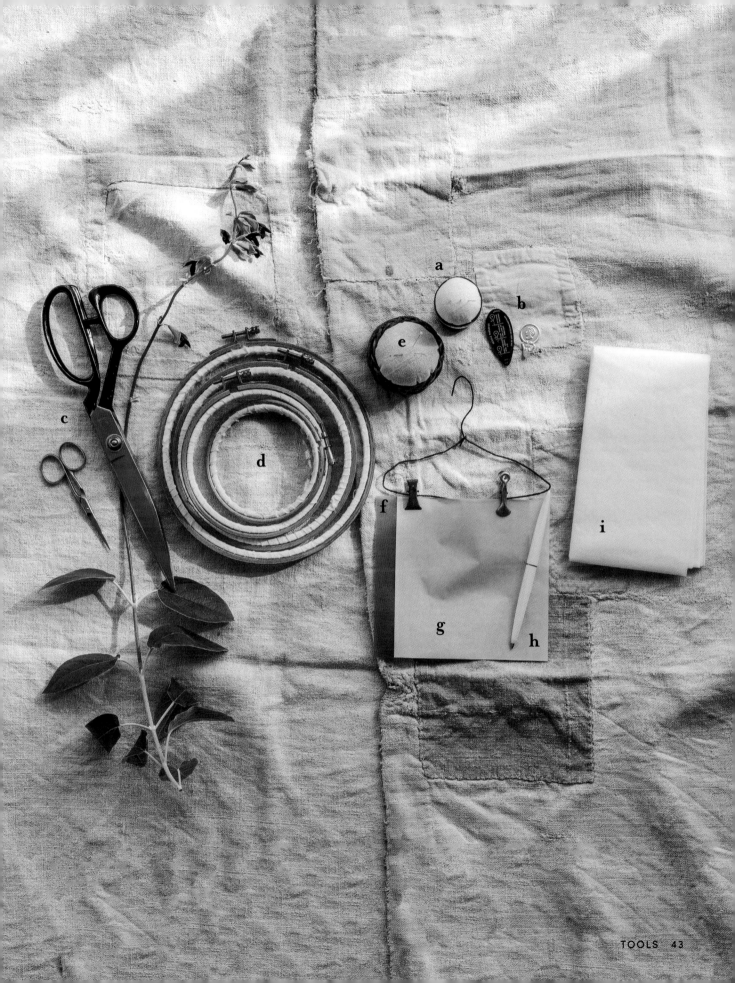

a

b

c

d

e

f

g

h

i

Getting Started

How to Transfer Embroidery Designs

When Using Carbon Chalk Paper

1. Align the tracing paper on top of the embroidery design (it may help to photocopy it from the book first so it is on a flat piece of paper). Use a pencil to trace the image.

2. Align the carbon chalk paper on top of the fabric (chalk side facing down). Layer the tracing paper on top and cover it with a sheet of cellophane. Use pins to secure the layers in place.

3. Trace the design using a tracer pen. The pressure on the pen will transfer the chalk onto the fabric in the shape of the embroidery design.

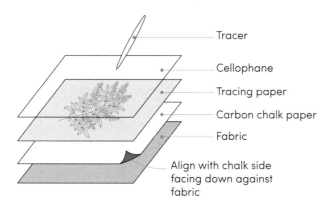

Tracer

Cellophane

Tracing paper

Carbon chalk paper

Fabric

Align with chalk side facing down against fabric

When Using Water Soluble Stabilizer

1. Align a sheet of water soluble stabilizer on top of the embroidery design. Use a water-based pen to trace the image.

2. Cut out the design. Align it on top of the fabric or object you wish to embroider. Baste or pin the design in place to secure and then embroider.

3. Once the embroidery is complete, remove the basting threads or pins.

4. Rinse under water to dissolve the water soluble stabilizer according to the manufacturer's instructions.

When Using Light

When working with light colored fabrics, you can use a sunny window or a light box to trace the embroidery design onto fabric. Make sure to use a pen that disappears with water or heat.

How to Read Embroidery Diagrams

The embroidery diagrams contain all the information you'll need to stitch the designs in this book. The following guide shows how to read the embroidery diagrams. Above each embroidery diagram, you'll also find some general notes that apply to the entire design.

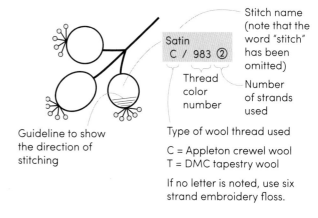

Satin
C / 983 ②

Stitch name (note that the word "stitch" has been omitted)

Thread color number

Number of strands used

Guideline to show the direction of stitching

Type of wool thread used

C = Appleton crewel wool
T = DMC tapestry wool

If no letter is noted, use six strand embroidery floss.

Wool Stitch Crest Motif

SHOWN ON PAGE 6

MATERIALS:

- DMC Tapestry Wool (1 skein each): 7196 (pink), 7260 (light pink), 7500 (light beige), and 7739 (cream)
- DMC Six Strand Embroidery Floss (1 skein each): 08 (brown), 310 (black), 829 (ocher), 895 (dark green), and 987 (green)

NOTES:

- Use satin stitch unless otherwise noted.
- Areas worked in tapestry wool are noted with a T. Use 1 strand of tapestry wool.
- Use six strand embroidery floss unless otherwise noted.

FULL-SIZE TEMPLATE:

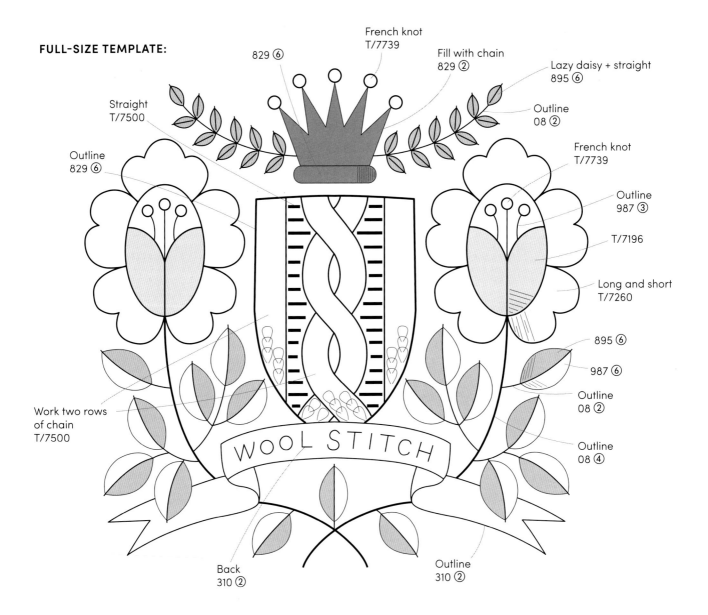

French knot
T/7739

829 ⑥

Fill with chain
829 ②

Lazy daisy + straight
895 ⑥

Straight
T/7500

Outline
08 ②

Outline
829 ⑥

French knot
T/7739

Outline
987 ③

T/7196

Long and short
T/7260

895 ⑥

987 ⑥

Outline
08 ②

Work two rows
of chain
T/7500

Outline
08 ④

Back
310 ②

Outline
310 ②

Wool Stitch Crest Pouch

SHOWN ON PAGE 7

MATERIALS:

- Outside fabric: 10" × 16" (25 × 40 cm) of white linen fabric
- Lining fabric: 10" × 16" (25 × 40 cm) of light pink linen fabric
- 4" (10 cm) of ¼" (5 mm) wide flat cord
- One ½" (1.3 cm) diameter shank button
- Thread: Refer to Wool Stitch Crest Motif on page 46
- Machine sewing thread to match fabric

CONSTRUCTION STEPS:

Sew using ⅜" (1 cm) seam allowance, unless otherwise noted.

1. Mark a 7" × 14¼" (18 × 36 cm) rectangle on the white linen fabric for the pouch outside. Next, add ⅜" (1 cm) to each edge for the seam allowance and mark. You'll also want to mark the bottom fold line. Transfer the embroidery template on page 46 onto the front of the pouch, following the placement noted in the diagram below. Embroider as noted, then trim the fabric along the marked seam allowance lines.

2. Cut a 8" × 15" (20 × 38 cm) rectangle of light pink linen fabric for the lining.

3. Fold a 2¾" (7 cm) piece of cord into a loop and pin to the right side of the embroidered pouch outside following the placement noted in the step 1 diagram. Align the pouch outside and lining with right sides together so the loop is sandwiched in between. Sew together along the top and bottom. Press the seams open.

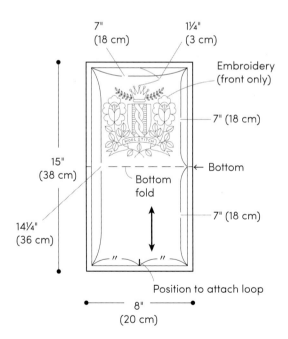

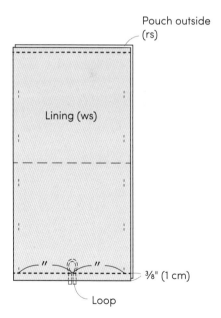

4. Fold both the pouch outside and lining in half along the bottom, centering the seams from step 3. Sew together along the left and right edges, leaving a 2¾" (7 cm) opening in the lining.

5. Turn right side out through the opening. Fold the opening seam allowances in and sew closed. Adjust the shape of the pouch, tucking the lining into the pouch outside. Sew the button to the front following the placement noted in the diagram below. The pouch will finish at 7" (18 cm) high × 7" (18 cm) wide.

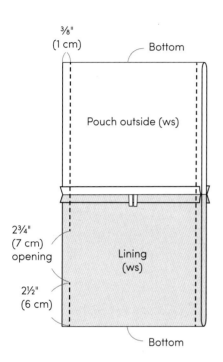

⅜"
(1 cm)

Bottom

Pouch outside (ws)

2¾"
(7 cm)
opening

Lining
(ws)

2½"
(6 cm)

Bottom

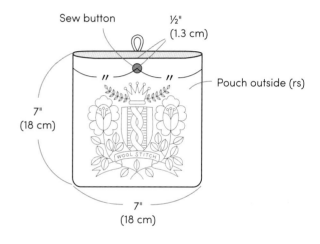

Sew button

½"
(1.3 cm)

Pouch outside (rs)

7"
(18 cm)

7"
(18 cm)

Botanical Garden Sampler

SHOWN ON PAGE 8

MATERIALS:

- DMC Tapestry Wool (1 skein each): ECRU (unbleached white), 7196 (pink), 7321 (light gray), 7327 (teal), 7385 (green), 7428 (moss green), 7452 (cream), 7473 (yellow), 7594 (light blue), 7702 (emerald green), 7758 (dark pink), and 7922 (orange)
- DMC Six Strand Embroidery Floss (1 skein each): ECRU (unbleached white), 319 (viridian), 500 (dark green), 502 (emerald green), 733 (mustard), 986 (green), 3346 (yellow green), and 3363 (grass green)

NOTES:

- Position the floral motifs on the fabric in a balanced way, using the photos on pages 8 and 9 as a guide.
- Use satin stitch unless otherwise noted.
- Areas worked in tapestry wool are noted with a T.
- Use six strand embroidery floss unless otherwise noted.

FULL-SIZE TEMPLATES:

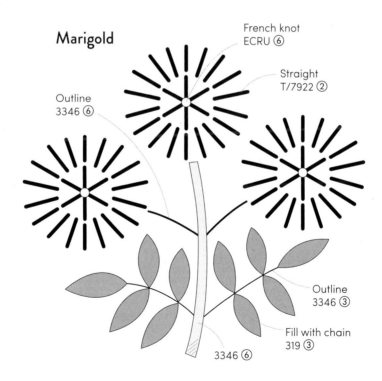

Marigold

French knot
ECRU ⑥

Straight
T/7922 ②

Outline
3346 ⑥

Outline
3346 ③

Fill with chain
319 ③

3346 ⑥

Elderflower

Rapeseed

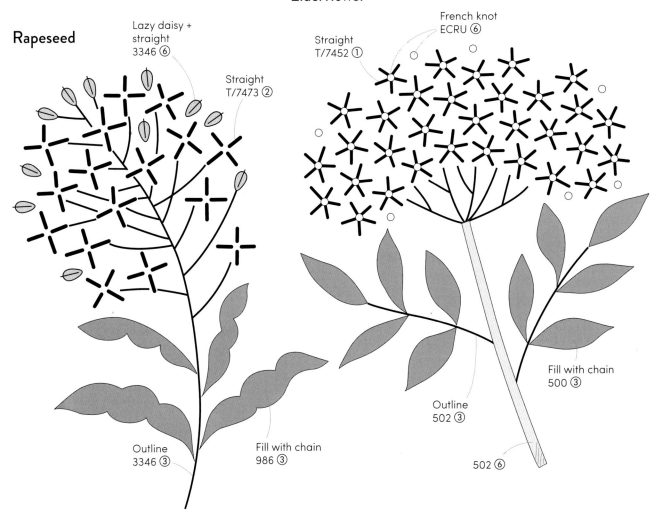

Lazy daisy +
straight
3346 ⑥

Straight
T/7473 ②

Outline
3346 ③

Fill with chain
986 ③

Straight
T/7452 ①

French knot
ECRU ⑥

Fill with chain
500 ③

Outline
502 ③

502 ⑥

Leaf

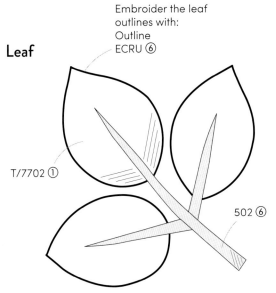

Embroider the leaf
outlines with:
Outline
ECRU ⑥

T/7702 ①

502 ⑥

Hydrangea

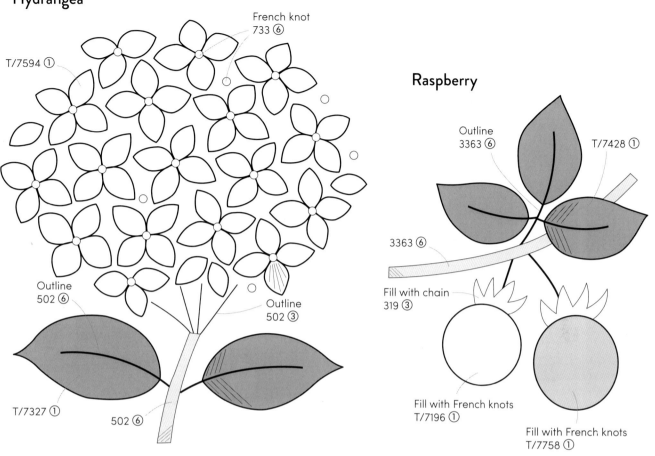

French knot
733 ⑥

T/7594 ①

Outline
502 ⑥

T/7327 ①

502 ⑥

Outline
502 ③

Raspberry

Outline
3363 ⑥

T/7428 ①

3363 ⑥

Fill with chain
319 ③

Fill with French knots
T/7196 ①

Fill with French knots
T/7758 ①

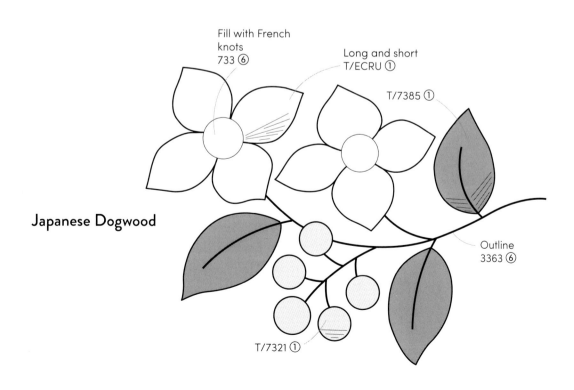

Fill with French
knots
733 ⑥

Long and short
T/ECRU ①

T/7385 ①

Japanese Dogwood

Outline
3363 ⑥

T/7321 ①

Mimosa Motif

SHOWN ON PAGE 10

MATERIALS:
- DMC Tapestry Wool (2 skeins): 7504 (yellow)
- DMC Six Strand Embroidery Floss (1 skein each): 320 (light green) and 505 (green)

NOTES:
- Position the floral motifs on the fabric in a balanced way, using the photo on page 10 as a guide.
- Areas worked in tapestry wool are noted with a T.
- Use six strand embroidery floss unless otherwise noted.

FULL-SIZE TEMPLATE:

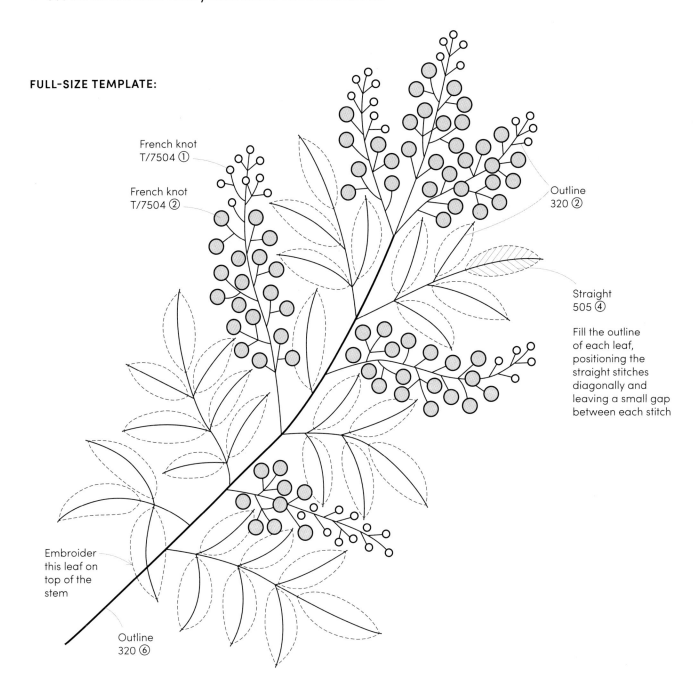

French knot
T/7504 ①

French knot
T/7504 ②

Outline
320 ②

Straight
505 ④

Fill the outline
of each leaf,
positioning the
straight stitches
diagonally and
leaving a small gap
between each stitch

Embroider
this leaf on
top of the
stem

Outline
320 ⑥

Mimosa Shawl

SHOWN ON PAGE 11

MATERIALS:

- One knit linen triangular shawl in beige
- Water soluble stabilizer
- Thread: Refer to Mimosa Motif on page 52

CONSTRUCTION STEPS:

1. Trace the template on page 52 onto the water soluble stabilizer (see page 45).

2. Position the stabilizer on top of the shawl following the placement noted in the diagram below. Pin or baste in place.

3. Embroider as noted on page 52.

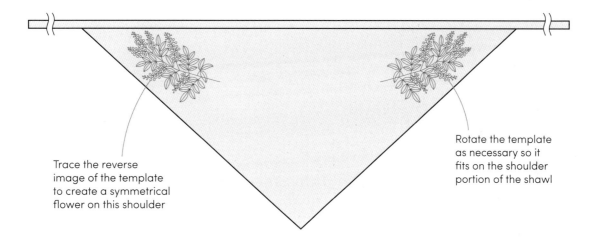

Trace the reverse image of the template to create a symmetrical flower on this shoulder

Rotate the template as necessary so it fits on the shoulder portion of the shawl

Flower Bed Motif

SHOWN ON PAGE 12

MATERIALS:
- Appleton Crewel Wool (1 skein each): 204 (light salmon pink), 206 (salmon pink), 866 (red orange), 964 (gray), and 991 (white)
- DMC Six Strand Embroidery Floss (1 skein each): 991 (emerald green) and 3816 (light emerald green)

NOTES:
- Overlap the template along the dashed lines to trace continuous repeats of the embroidery motif.
- Use long and short stitch unless otherwise noted.
- Areas worked in crewel wool are noted with a C.
- Use six strand embroidery floss unless otherwise noted.

FULL-SIZE TEMPLATE:

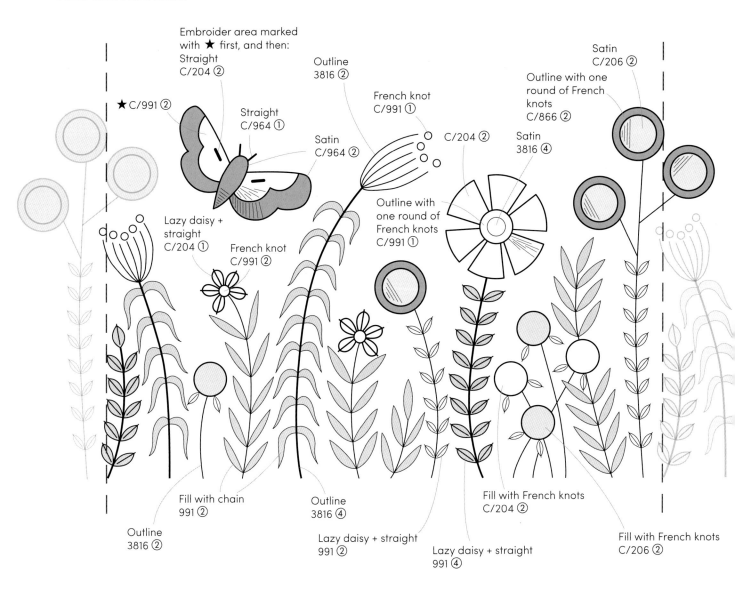

Embroider area marked with ★ first, and then:
Straight C/204 ②

★ C/991 ②

Straight C/964 ①

Outline 3816 ②

French knot C/991 ①

C/204 ②

Satin C/206 ②

Outline with one round of French knots C/866 ②

Satin 3816 ④

Satin C/964 ②

Lazy daisy + straight C/204 ①

French knot C/991 ②

Outline with one round of French knots C/991 ①

Fill with chain 991 ②

Outline 3816 ②

Outline 3816 ④

Lazy daisy + straight 991 ②

Fill with French knots C/204 ②

Lazy daisy + straight 991 ④

Fill with French knots C/206 ②

Flower Rhythm Motif

SHOWN ON PAGE 13

MATERIALS:
- DMC Tapestry Wool (1 skein): 7127 (red brown)
- DMC Six Strand Embroidery Floss (1 skein each): 500 (dark green) and 561 (emerald green)

NOTES:
- Overlap the template along the dashed lines to trace continuous repeats of the embroidery motif.
- Areas worked in tapestry wool are noted with a T.
- Use six strand embroidery floss unless otherwise noted.

FULL-SIZE TEMPLATE:

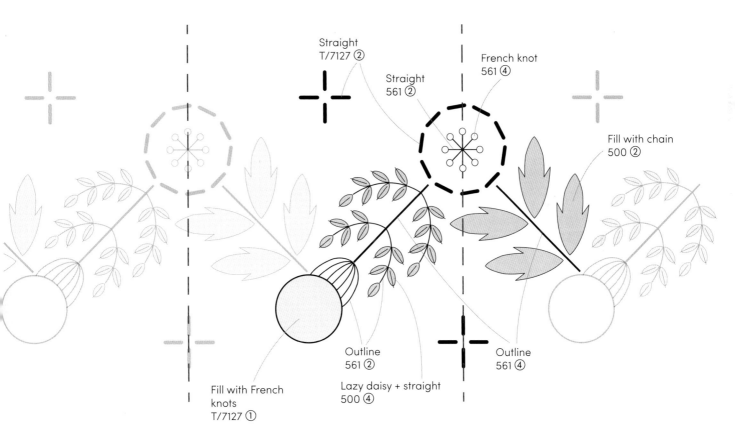

Straight
T/7127 ②

Straight
561 ②

French knot
561 ④

Fill with chain
500 ②

Outline
561 ②

Outline
561 ④

Fill with French
knots
T/7127 ①

Lazy daisy + straight
500 ④

Butterflies Motif

SHOWN ON PAGE 14

FULL-SIZE TEMPLATE:

MATERIALS:

- Appleton Crewel Wool (1 skein each): 477 (orange), 743 (blue), 844 (yellow), 921 (blue gray), 991 (white), and 993 (black)
- DMC Six Strand Embroidery Floss (1 skein each): 310 (black) and 3866 (off-white)

NOTES:

- Use satin stitch unless otherwise noted.
- Use 1 strand unless otherwise noted.
- Areas worked in crewel wool are noted with a C.
- Use six strand embroidery floss unless otherwise noted.

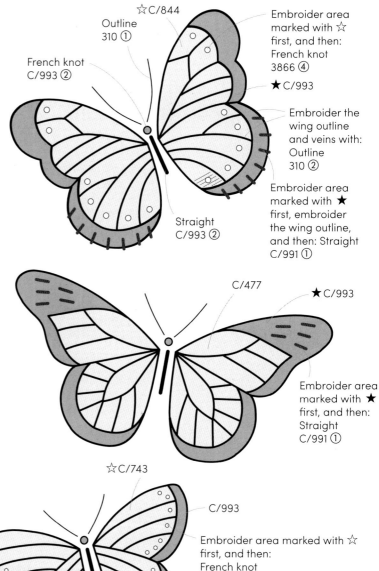

☆C/844

Outline 310 ①

French knot C/993 ②

Embroider area marked with ☆ first, and then: French knot 3866 ④

★C/993

Embroider the wing outline and veins with: Outline 310 ②

Embroider area marked with ★ first, embroider the wing outline, and then: Straight C/991 ①

Straight C/993 ②

C/477

★C/993

Embroider area marked with ★ first, and then: Straight C/991 ①

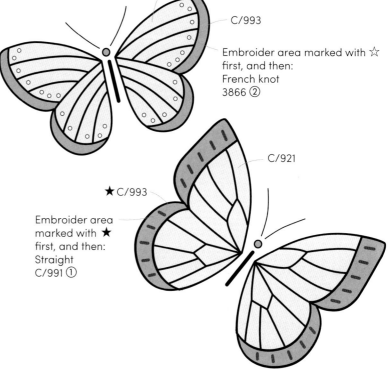

☆C/743

C/993

Embroider area marked with ☆ first, and then: French knot 3866 ②

C/921

★C/993

Embroider area marked with ★ first, and then: Straight C/991 ①

Butterfly Beret

SHOWN ON PAGE 15

MATERIALS:

- Appleton Crewel Wool (1 skein each): 844 (yellow), 991 (white), and 993 (black)
- DMC Six Strand Embroidery Floss (1 skein each): 310 (black) and 3866 (off-white)
- Beige felt beret
- Water soluble stabilizer

CONSTRUCTION STEPS:

1. Trace the embroidery motif onto water soluble stabilizer (see page 45).

2. Position the stabilizer on the beret as desired. Pin or baste in place.

3. Embroider the motif as noted. If the beret can't be placed into an embroidery hoop, just hold the hat as you stitch.

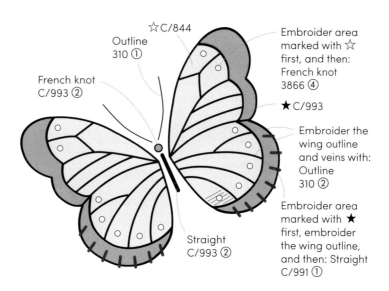

☆C/844

Outline 310 ①

French knot C/993 ②

Embroider area marked with ☆ first, and then: French knot 3866 ④

★C/993

Embroider the wing outline and veins with: Outline 310 ②

Embroider area marked with ★ first, embroider the wing outline, and then: Straight C/991 ①

Straight C/993 ②

Thistle Wreath Motif

SHOWN ON PAGE 16

MATERIALS:
- DMC Tapestry Wool (1 skein each): 707 (magenta), 708 (purple), 7251 (light pink), and 7702 (green)
- DMC Six Strand Embroidery Floss (1 skein each): 319 (viridian) and 3363 (grass green)

NOTES:
- Areas worked in tapestry wool are noted with a T.
- Use six strand embroidery floss unless otherwise noted.

FULL-SIZE TEMPLATE:

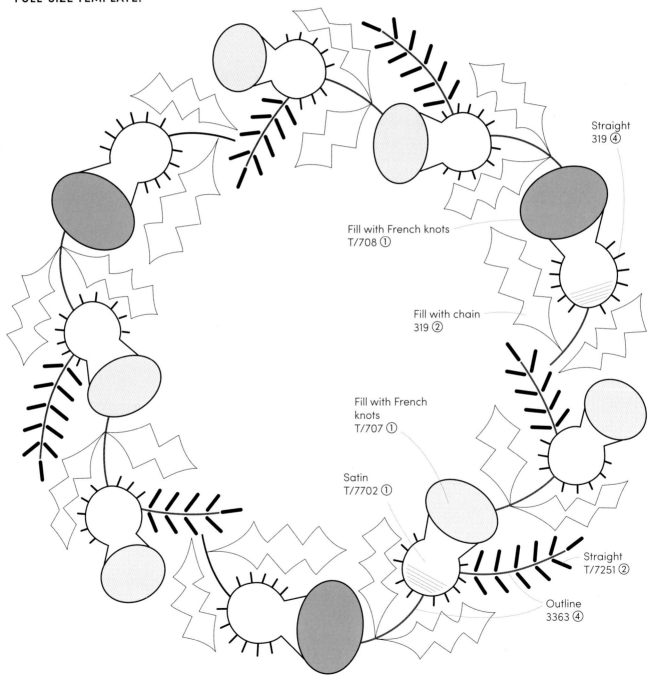

Straight
319 ④

Fill with French knots
T/708 ①

Fill with chain
319 ②

Fill with French
knots
T/707 ①

Satin
T/7702 ①

Straight
T/7251 ②

Outline
3363 ④

Thistle Wreath Pot Mat

SHOWN ON PAGE 17

MATERIALS:
- Fabric: 15" × 25" (38 × 63.5 cm) of white linen fabric
- Thread: Refer to Thistle Wreath Motif on page 58
- Machine sewing thread to match fabric

CONSTRUCTION STEPS:

Sew using ⅜" (1 cm) seam allowance, unless otherwise noted.

1. Cut a 15" (38 cm) square of white linen fabric for the front. Mark a 8¼" (21 cm) circle. Next, add ⅜" (1 cm) for the seam allowance and mark. Transfer the embroidery template on page 58 onto the fabric, following the placement noted in the diagram below. Embroider as noted, then trim the fabric along the marked seam allowance lines.

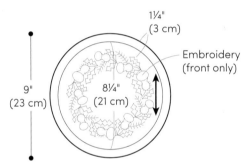

2. Cut a 9" (23 cm) circle of white linen fabric for the back. Align the front and the back with right sides together. Sew, leaving a 2" (5 cm) opening to turn right side out.

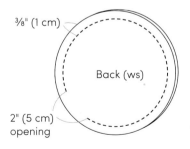

3. Trim the seam allowance to ¼" (5 mm) and make clips, being careful not to cut through the stitching.

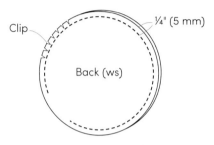

4. Turn right side out through the opening. Fold the seam allowances in and sew closed. The pot mat will finish at 8¼" (21 cm) in diameter.

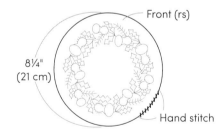

Vintage Flower Pattern

SHOWN ON PAGE 18

MATERIALS:

- DMC Tapestry Wool (1 skein each): 7398 (deep green), 7500 (light beige), 7702 (emerald green), and 7739 (cream)
- DMC Six Strand Embroidery Floss (1 skein each): 839 (brown) and 3045 (ocher)

NOTES:

- Overlap the template along the dashed lines to trace continuous repeats of the embroidery motif.
- Use straight stitch unless otherwise noted.
- Areas worked in tapestry wool are noted with a T.
- Use six strand embroidery floss unless otherwise noted.

FULL-SIZE TEMPLATE:

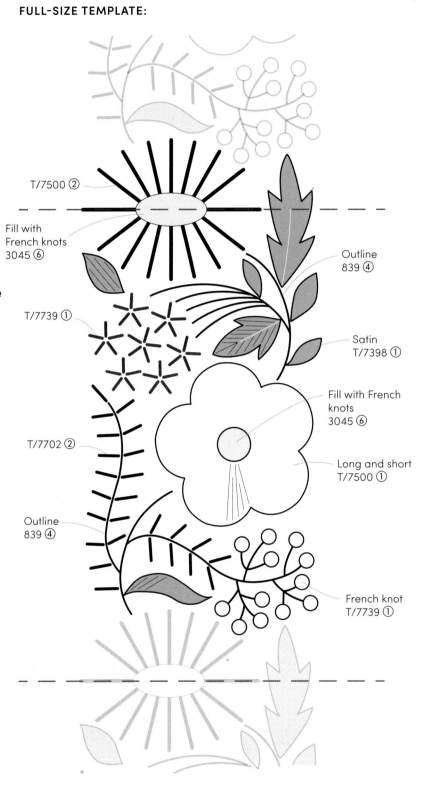

T/7500 ②

Fill with French knots 3045 ⑥

T/7739 ①

T/7702 ②

Outline 839 ④

Outline 839 ④

Satin T/7398 ①

Fill with French knots 3045 ⑥

Long and short T/7500 ①

French knot T/7739 ①

Tile Pin Cushions

SHOWN ON PAGE 19

MATERIALS (FOR ONE PIN CUSHION):

- Front fabric: 8" × 8" (20 × 20 cm) of navy (for a and c) or white (for b) linen fabric
- Appleton Crewel Wool (1 skein each): 991 (white) for a and c or 749 (dark blue) for b
- DMC Six Strand Embroidery Floss (1 skein each): 3866 (off-white) for a and c or 336 (dark blue) for b
- Polyester stuffing
- Machine sewing thread to match fabric

NOTES:

- Areas worked in crewel wool are noted with a C. Use 2 strands of crewel wool.
- Use six strand embroidery floss unless otherwise noted.

FULL-SIZE TEMPLATES:

a

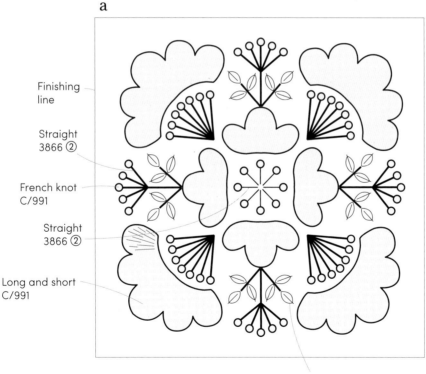

Finishing line

Straight 3866 ②

French knot C/991

Straight 3866 ②

Long and short C/991

Lazy daisy + straight 3866 ④

b

French knot
C/749

Finishing line

Outline
336 ②

Lazy daisy + straight
C/749

Straight
336 ②

Long and short
C/749

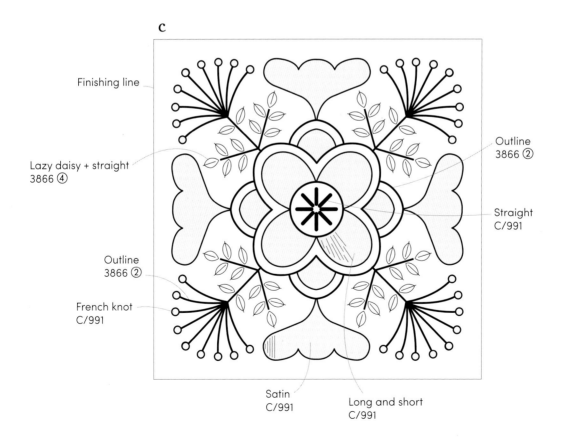

c

Finishing line

Lazy daisy + straight
3866 ④

Outline
3866 ②

French knot
C/991

Outline
3866 ②

Straight
C/991

Satin
C/991

Long and short
C/991

CONSTRUCTION STEPS:

Sew using ⅜" (1 cm) seam allowance, unless otherwise noted.

1. Mark a 3½" (9 cm) square on the linen fabric for the front. Next, add ⅜" (1 cm) to each edge for the seam allowance and mark. Transfer the desired embroidery template from page 61 or 62 onto the front, following the placement noted in the diagram below. Embroider as noted, then trim the fabric along the marked seam allowance lines.

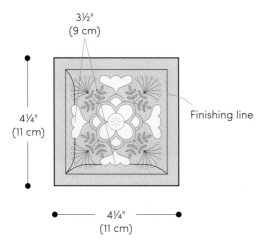

3½"
(9 cm)

4¼"
(11 cm)

Finishing line

4¼"
(11 cm)

2. Cut a 4¼" (11 cm) square of linen fabric for the back. Align the front and the back with right sides together. Sew, leaving a 2" (5 cm) opening to turn right side out.

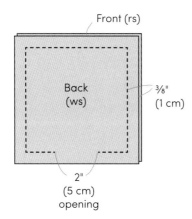

Front (rs)

Back
(ws)

⅜"
(1 cm)

2"
(5 cm)
opening

3. Trim the seam allowance to ¼" (5 mm) and clip the corners, being careful not to cut through the stitching.

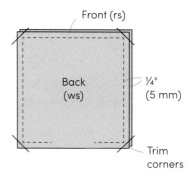

Front (rs)

Back
(ws)

¼"
(5 mm)

Trim
corners

4. Turn right side out through the opening. Fill with polyester stuffing. Fold the seam allowances in and sew closed. The pin cushions will finish at 3½" (9 cm) square.

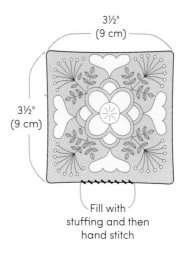

3½"
(9 cm)

3½"
(9 cm)

Fill with
stuffing and then
hand stitch

Botanical Garden Cushion

SHOWN ON PAGE 20

MATERIALS:

- Fabric: 30" × 16" (75 × 40 cm) of black linen fabric
- One 12" × 12" (30 × 30 cm) pillow insert
- Thread: Refer to Botanical Garden Sampler on page 49
- Machine sewing thread to match fabric

CONSTRUCTION STEPS:

Sew using ⅜" (1 cm) seam allowance, unless otherwise noted.

1. Mark a 26" × 11¾" (66 × 30 cm) rectangle on the black linen fabric. Next, add 1" (2.5 cm) to the top and bottom edges and ¾" (2 cm) to the left and right edges for the seam allowance and mark. You'll also want to mark the fold lines. Transfer the embroidery templates on pages 49–51 onto the fabric, positioning the individual motifs in a balanced manner (refer to the photo on page 20 as a guide). Embroider as noted, then trim the fabric along the marked seam allowance lines.

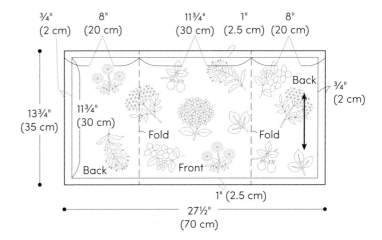

2. Fold and press the left and right edges over ⅜" (1 cm) twice. Topstitch, stitching 1⁄16" (2 mm) from the edge.

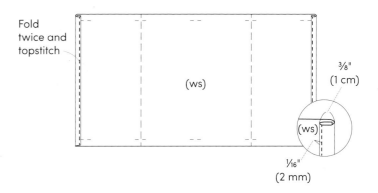

3. Fold with wrong sides together along the lines marked in step 1 so the two sections overlap at the back. Sew together along the top and bottom using ⅜" (1 cm) seam allowance.

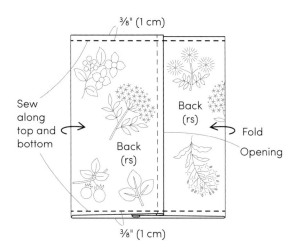

⅜" (1 cm)

Sew along top and bottom

Back (rs)

Back (rs)

Fold

Opening

⅜" (1 cm)

4. Turn the cushion inside out. Sew together along the top and bottom again using ⅝" (1.5 cm) seam allowance this time.

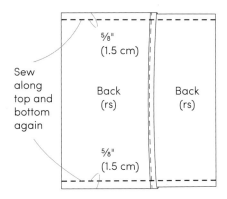

Sew along top and bottom again

⅝" (1.5 cm)

Back (rs)

Back (rs)

⅝" (1.5 cm)

5. Turn the cushion right side out and adjust the shape of the corners. Insert the pillow form. The cushion will finish at 12" (30 cm) tall × 12" (30 cm) wide.

Poppy Sampler

SHOWN ON PAGE 21

MATERIALS:

- Fabric: 14" × 14" (35 × 35 cm) of cream linen
- Appleton Crewel Wool (1 skein each): 181 (light pink), 206 (salmon pink), 311 (mustard yellow), 331 (light yellow), 477 (orange), 602 (light purple), and 991 (white)
- DMC Six Strand Embroidery Floss (1 skein each unless otherwise noted): 320 (light green), 918 (rust red), and 561 (emerald green, 2 skeins)
- One 8" (20 cm) diameter embroidery hoop
- 6" (15 cm) square of brown felt
- Brown hand sewing thread

CONSTRUCTION STEPS:

1. Transfer the template on page 67 onto the fabric. Embroider as noted. Insert into the hoop, positioning the embroidery as desired.

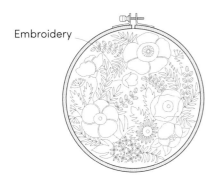

Embroidery

2. Trim the excess fabric, leaving 2½" (6–7 cm). Use hand sewing thread to running stitch along the fabric about 2" (5 cm) from the hoop. Leave long thread tails. Pull the thread tails to gather the fabric. Sew a couple of overlapping stitches, and then knot to secure.

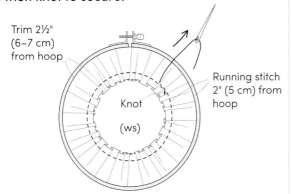

Trim 2½" (6–7 cm) from hoop

Knot

(ws)

Running stitch 2" (5 cm) from hoop

3. Cut a 4¾" (12 cm) diameter felt circle. Position on the wrong side of the hoop so the felt hides the running stitches from step 3. Hand sew the felt to the fabric.

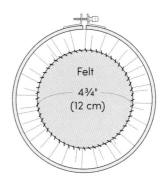

Felt
4¾"
(12 cm)

NOTES:

- Use long and short stitch unless otherwise noted. Use 2 strands.
- Areas worked in crewel wool are noted with a C.
- Use six strand embroidery floss unless otherwise noted.

FULL-SIZE TEMPLATE:

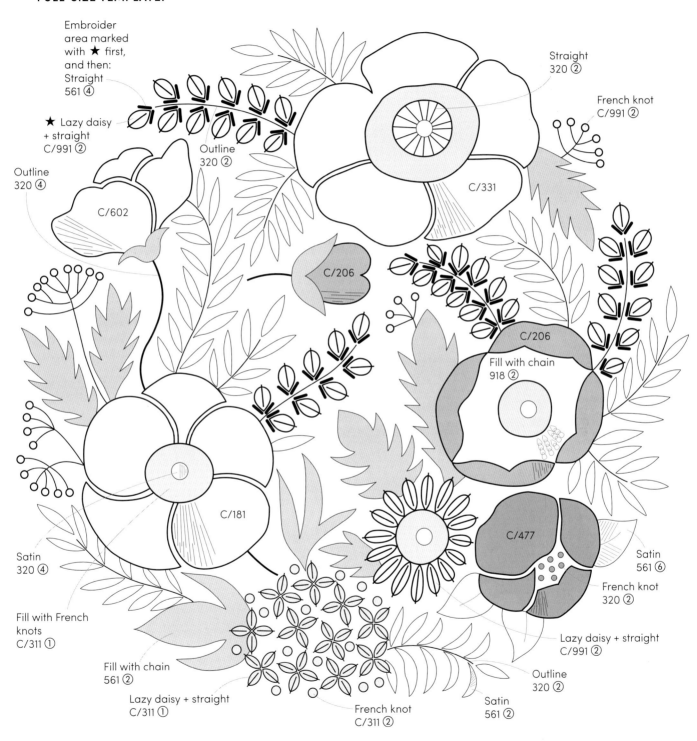

Embroider area marked with ★ first, and then: Straight 561 ④

★ Lazy daisy + straight C/991 ②

Outline 320 ④

C/602

Outline 320 ②

Straight 320 ②

French knot C/991 ②

C/331

C/206

C/206

Fill with chain 918 ②

C/181

C/477

Satin 561 ⑥

French knot 320 ②

Satin 320 ④

Fill with French knots C/311 ①

Fill with chain 561 ②

Lazy daisy + straight C/311 ①

French knot C/311 ②

Satin 561 ②

Lazy daisy + straight C/991 ②

Outline 320 ②

Dandelion Motif

SHOWN ON PAGE 22

MATERIALS:
- DMC Tapestry Wool (1 skein each): 7385 (green) and 7473 (yellow)
- DMC Six Strand Embroidery Floss (1 skein each): 18 (yellow) and 3364 (light green)

NOTES:
- Position the floral motifs on the fabric in a balanced way, using the photo on page 22 as a guide.
- Areas worked in tapestry wool are noted with a T.
- Use six strand embroidery floss unless otherwise noted.

FULL-SIZE TEMPLATE:

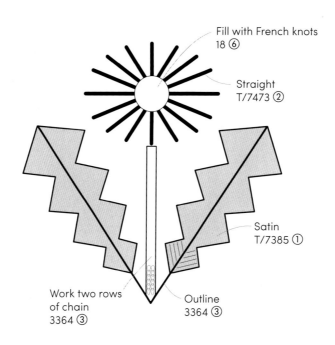

Fill with French knots
18 ⑥

Straight
T/7473 ②

Satin
T/7385 ①

Work two rows
of chain
3364 ③

Outline
3364 ③

Modern Flower Motif

SHOWN ON PAGE 23

MATERIALS:

- DMC Tapestry Wool (1 skein each): 7010 (salmon pink), 7121 (light pink), 7385 (green), 7404 (light green), 7500 (light beige), and 7518 (light brown)
- DMC Six Strand Embroidery Floss (1 skein each): 356 (light pink) and 986 (green)
- **Note:** If you plan on embroidering this motif onto a knit garment as shown on page 23, you'll also need water soluble stabilizer.

NOTES:

- Use long and short stitch unless otherwise noted. Use 1 strand.
- Areas worked in tapestry wool are noted with a T.
- Use six strand embroidery floss unless otherwise noted.

FULL-SIZE TEMPLATE:

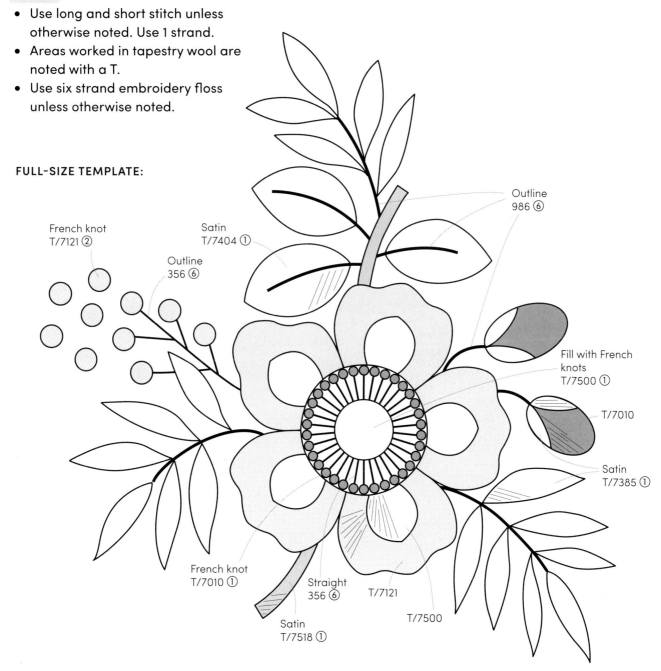

Pressed Flowers Motif

SHOWN ON PAGE 24

MATERIALS:

- Appleton Crewel Wool (1 skein each): 105 (purple), 106 (dark purple), 311 (yellow), 603 (light purple), 605 (grape), 741 (periwinkle), 834 (green), and 991 (white)
- DMC Six Strand Embroidery Floss (1 skein): 505 (green)

STITCH GUIDE (NOT A TEMPLATE):

- ▲ = Long and short stitch (2 strands)   ★ = Satin stitch
- △ = French knots   ☆ = Lazy daisy stitch + straight stitch
- Areas worked in crewel wool are noted with a C.
- Use six strand embroidery floss unless otherwise noted.

Pressed Flowers Tote

SHOWN ON PAGE 25

MATERIALS:

- Outside/handle fabric: 22" × 38" (55 x 95 cm) of black linen fabric
- Lining fabric: 20" × 38" (50 x 95 cm) of navy blue linen fabric
- Thread: Refer to Pressed Flowers Motif on page 70
- Machine sewing thread to match fabric

CONSTRUCTION STEPS:

1. Mark a 17¾" × 35½" (45 x 90 cm) rectangle on the black linen fabric for the bag outside. Next, add ⅜" (1 cm) to each edge for the seam allowance and mark. You'll also want to mark the bottom fold line and the handle placement. Transfer the embroidery templates on page 71 onto the front of the bag, positioning the individual floral motifs in a balanced manner. Embroider as noted, then trim the fabric along the marked seam allowance lines.

2. Cut a 18½" × 36¼" (47 x 92 cm) rectangle of navy blue linen fabric for the lining.

3. Cut two 2" × 17¾" (5 x 45 cm) rectangles of black linen fabric for the handles.

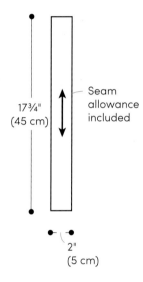

17¾" (45 cm)

Seam allowance included

2" (5 cm)

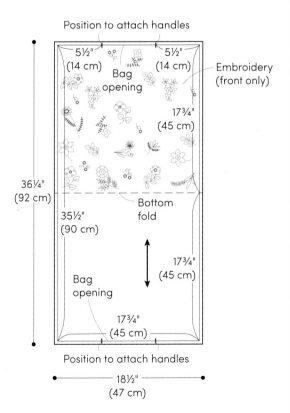

Position to attach handles

5½" (14 cm)   5½" (14 cm)

Bag opening

Embroidery (front only)

17¾" (45 cm)

36¼" (92 cm)

35½" (90 cm)

Bottom fold

17¾" (45 cm)

Bag opening

17¾" (45 cm)

Position to attach handles

18½" (47 cm)

4. Fold each handle in half and press. Open flat and then fold the edges in to meet the center crease. Press. Fold in half again and press. Topstitch each long edge.

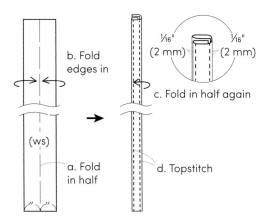

b. Fold edges in

$\frac{1}{16}$" (2 mm) $\frac{1}{16}$" (2 mm)

c. Fold in half again

(ws)

a. Fold in half

d. Topstitch

5. Align each handle with the right side of the bag outside following the placement marked in step 1. Baste to secure the handles in place. Align the bag outside and lining with right sides together so the handles are sandwiched in between. Sew together along the top and bottom. Press the seams open.

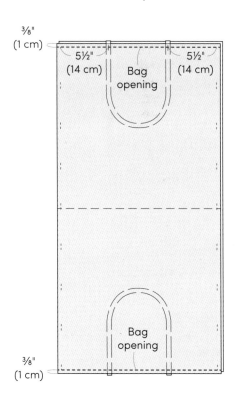

$\frac{3}{8}$" (1 cm)

5½" (14 cm)   Bag opening   5½" (14 cm)

Bag opening

$\frac{3}{8}$" (1 cm)

6. Fold both the bag outside and lining in half along the bottom, centering the seams from step 5. Sew together along the left and right edges, leaving a 2¾" (7 cm) opening in the lining.

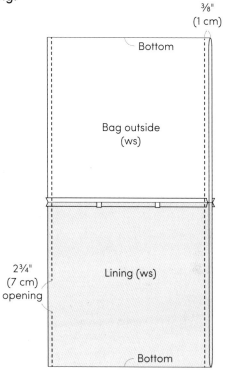

$\frac{3}{8}$" (1 cm)

Bottom

Bag outside (ws)

2¾" (7 cm) opening

Lining (ws)

Bottom

7. Turn right side out through the opening. Fold the opening seam allowances in and sew closed. Adjust the shape of the bag, tucking the lining into the bag outside. The tote will finish at 17¾" (45 cm) tall × 17¾" (45 cm) wide, not including the handles.

Bag outside (rs)

Bird Paradise Motif

SHOWN ON PAGE 26

MATERIALS:

- Appleton Crewel Wool (1 skein each): 181 (light pink), 562 (light blue), 564 (medium blue), 566 (dark blue), 641 (light green), 833 (green), 835 (dark green), 944 (pink), and 995 (red)
- DMC Six Strand Embroidery Floss (1 skein): 319 (viridian), 733 (mustard), and 3363 (grass green)

STITCH GUIDE (NOT A TEMPLATE):

- Use long and short stitch unless otherwise noted. Use 2 strands.
- Areas worked in crewel wool are noted with a C.
- Use six strand embroidery floss unless otherwise noted.

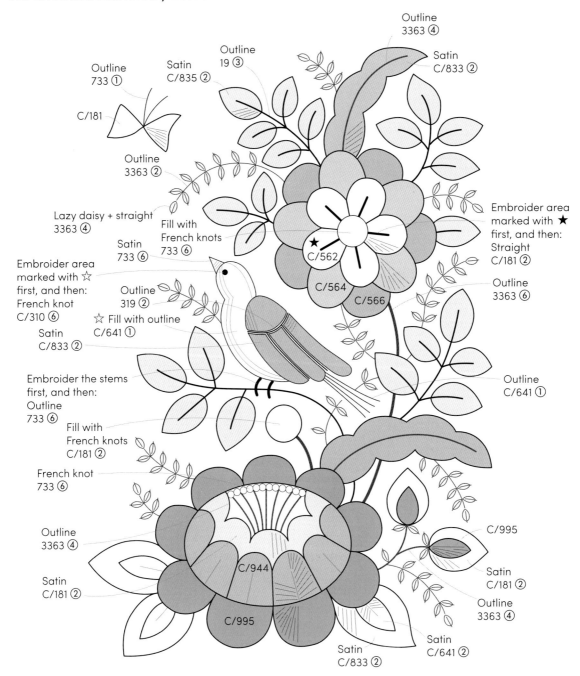

Outline 3363 ④

Satin C/833 ②

Outline 19 ③

Satin C/835 ②

Outline 733 ①

C/181

Outline 3363 ②

Embroider area marked with ★ first, and then: Straight C/181 ②

Lazy daisy + straight 3363 ④

Fill with French knots 733 ⑥

Satin 733 ⑥

C/562

C/564

C/566

Outline 3363 ⑥

Embroider area marked with ☆ first, and then: French knot C/310 ⑥

Outline 319 ②

☆ Fill with outline C/641 ①

Satin C/833 ②

Embroider the stems first, and then: Outline 733 ⑥

Outline C/641 ①

Fill with French knots C/181 ②

French knot 733 ⑥

C/995

Outline 3363 ④

Satin C/181 ②

C/944

C/995

Satin C/181 ②

Outline 3363 ④

Satin C/641 ②

Satin C/833 ②

Funny Flower Pattern

SHOWN ON PAGE 27

MATERIALS:

- Appleton Crewel Wool (1 skein each): 528 (emerald green), 753 (pink), 863 (orange), 866 (red orange), 946 (magenta), and 991 (white)
- DMC Six Strand Embroidery Floss (1 skein): 3813 (pale green)

NOTES:

- Position the floral motifs on the fabric in a balanced way, using the photo on page 27 as a guide.
- Areas worked in crewel wool are noted with a C.
- Use six strand embroidery floss unless otherwise noted.

FULL-SIZE TEMPLATE:

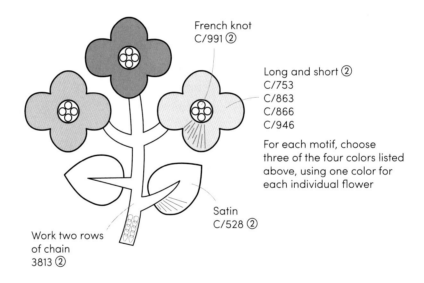

French knot
C/991 ②

Long and short ②
C/753
C/863
C/866
C/946

For each motif, choose three of the four colors listed above, using one color for each individual flower

Satin
C/528 ②

Work two rows
of chain
3813 ②

Pansy Motif

SHOWN ON PAGE 28

MATERIALS:

- DMC Tapestry Wool (1 skein each): 7022 (purple), 7023 (deep purple), 7244 (light purple), 7284 (light blue), 7307 (navy), 7510 (light gray), 7540 (green), 7555 (blue gray), and 7739 (cream)
- DMC Six Strand Embroidery Floss (1 skein): 3347 (yellow green)

NOTES:

- Use long and short stitch unless otherwise noted. Use 1 strand.
- Areas worked in tapestry wool are noted with a T.
- Use six strand embroidery floss unless otherwise noted.

FULL-SIZE TEMPLATE:

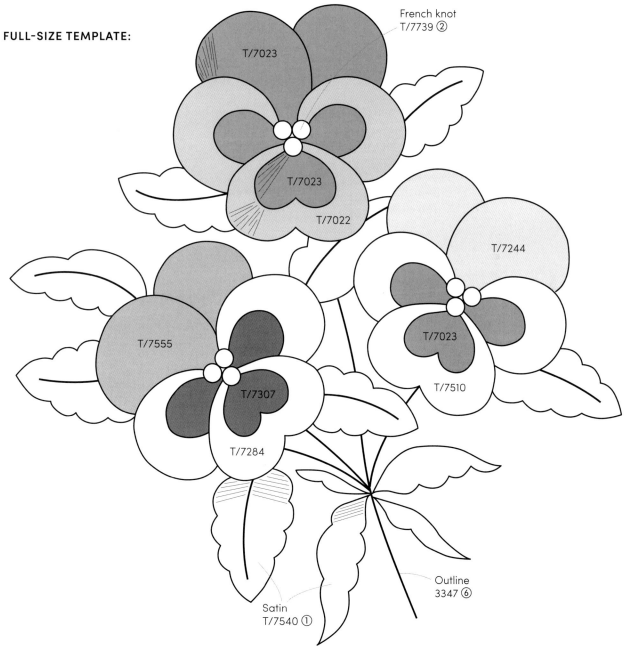

French knot
T/7739 ②

T/7023

T/7023

T/7022

T/7244

T/7555

T/7023

T/7307

T/7510

T/7284

Outline
3347 ⑥

Satin
T/7540 ①

Pansy Tote

SHOWN ON PAGE 29

MATERIALS:

- Outside/handle fabric: 18" × 29½" (45 × 75 cm) of white linen fabric
- Lining fabric: 14" × 29½" (35 × 75 cm) of gray linen fabric
- Thread: Refer to Pansy Motif on page 77
- Machine sewing thread to match fabric

CONSTRUCTION STEPS:

Sew using ⅜" (1 cm) seam allowance, unless otherwise noted.

1. Mark a 10¾" × 26" (27 × 66 cm) rectangle on the white linen fabric for the bag outside. Next, add ⅜" (1 cm) to each edge for the seam allowance and mark. You'll also want to mark the bottom fold line and the handle placement. Transfer the embroidery template on page 77 onto the front of the bag, following the placement shown in the diagram below. Embroider as noted, then trim the fabric along the marked seam allowance lines.

2. Cut a 11½" × 26¾" (29 × 68 cm) rectangle of gray linen fabric for the lining.

3. Cut two 2" × 24½" (5 × 62 cm) rectangles of white linen fabric for the handles.

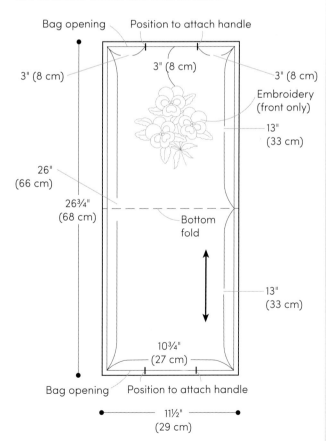

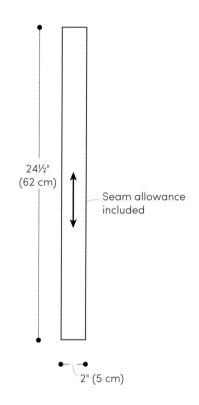

4. Follow steps 4–7 on page 73 to assemble the tote bag. The tote will finish at 13" (33 cm) tall × 10¾" (27 cm) wide, not including the handles.

Classical Flower Sampler

SHOWN ON PAGE 30

MATERIALS:

- Fabric: 14" × 14" (35 × 35 cm) of light blue linen
- DMC Tapestry Wool (1 skein each): ECRU (unbleached white), 7194 (pink), 7221 (light pink), 7398 (deep green), 7540 (green), and 7758 (dark pink)
- DMC Six Strand Embroidery Floss (1 skein each): 733 (mustard), 890 (green), 3363 (grass green), and 3790 (brown)
- One 8" (20 cm) diameter embroidery hoop
- 6" (15 cm) square of blue felt
- Blue hand sewing thread
- **Note:** See page 66 for instructions for mounting the sampler in an embroidery hoop.

NOTES:

- Use long and short stitch unless otherwise noted.
- Areas worked in tapestry wool are noted with a T. Use 1 strand.
- Use six strand embroidery floss unless otherwise noted.

FULL-SIZE TEMPLATE:

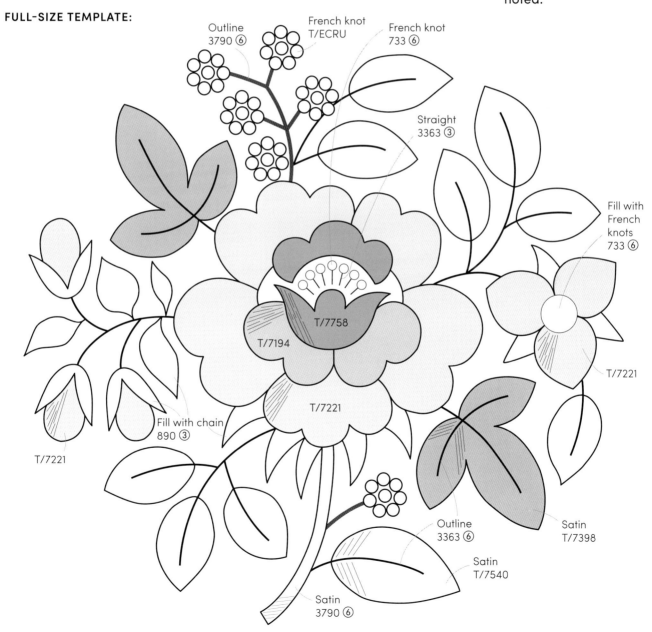

Flower River Ribbon

SHOWN ON PAGE 31

MATERIALS:

- Appleton Crewel Wool (1 skein each): 644 (light green), 834 (green), 843 (yellow), 863 (orange), 866 (red orange), 941 (light pink), 946 (pink), 948 (dark red), 964 (gray), and 991 (white)
- DMC Six Strand Embroidery Floss (1 skein): 500 (deep green)
- 38½" (98 cm) of 2½" (6 cm) wide beige flatweave ribbon

NOTES:

- Overlap the template along the dashed lines to trace continuous repeats of the embroidery motif.
- Use outline stitch in 500 ⑥ unless otherwise noted.
- Areas worked in crewel wool are noted with a C.
- Use six strand embroidery floss unless otherwise noted.

FULL-SIZE TEMPLATE:

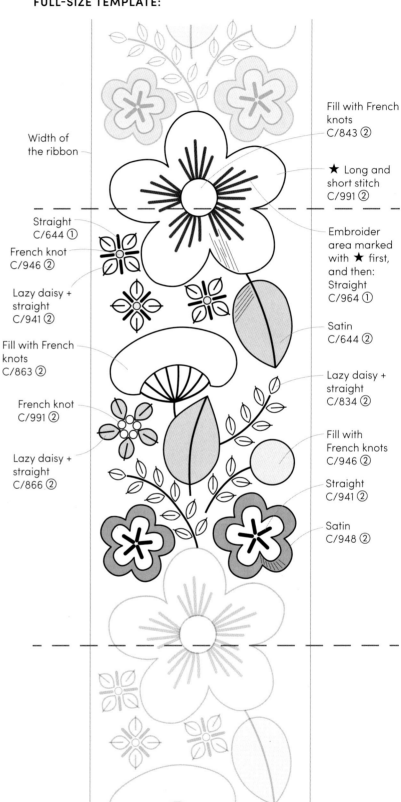

Width of the ribbon

Fill with French knots C/843 ②

★ Long and short stitch C/991 ②

Embroider area marked with ★ first, and then: Straight C/964 ①

Satin C/644 ②

Lazy daisy + straight C/834 ②

Fill with French knots C/946 ②

Straight C/941 ②

Satin C/948 ②

Straight C/644 ①

French knot C/946 ②

Lazy daisy + straight C/941 ②

Fill with French knots C/863 ②

French knot C/991 ②

Lazy daisy + straight C/866 ②

Small Berries Motif

SHOWN ON PAGE 32

MATERIALS:

- Appleton Crewel Wool (1 skein each): 833 (green) and 991 (white)
- DMC Six Strand Embroidery Floss (1 skein): 08 (brown)

NOTES:

- Position the floral motifs on the fabric in a balanced way, using the photo on page 32 as a guide.
- Areas worked in crewel wool are noted with a C.
- Use six strand embroidery floss unless otherwise noted.

FULL-SIZE TEMPLATE:

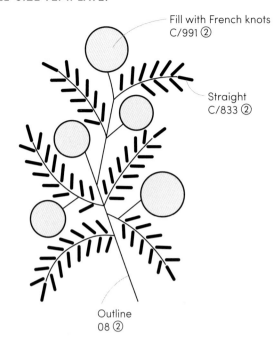

Fill with French knots
C/991 ②

Straight
C/833 ②

Outline
08 ②

Small Berries Shawl

This motif is perfect for embellishing a store bought shawl, such as the wool shawl shown on page 33. Simply follow these steps:

1. Trace the embroidery motif onto water soluble stabilizer (see page 45).

2. Position the stabilizer on top of the shawl, randomly scattering the flower motifs (use the photo on page 33 as a guide). Pin or baste it place.

3. Embroider the motif as noted.

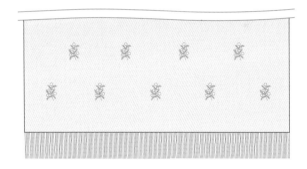

Mushroom Sampler

SHOWN ON PAGE 36

MATERIALS:
- Fabric: 14" × 12" (35 × 30 cm) of black linen
- Appleton Crewel Wool (1 skein each): 723 (red), 976 (brown), 983 (dark beige), and 986 (chestnut brown)
- DMC Six Strand Embroidery Floss (1 skein each): 07 (dark beige), 895 (dark green), 3031 (dark brown), and 3866 (off-white)
- One 12" × 10" (30 × 26 cm) frame

NOTES:
- Use outline stitch unless otherwise noted.
- Areas worked in crewel wool are noted with a C.
- Use six strand embroidery floss unless otherwise noted.

FULL-SIZE TEMPLATE:

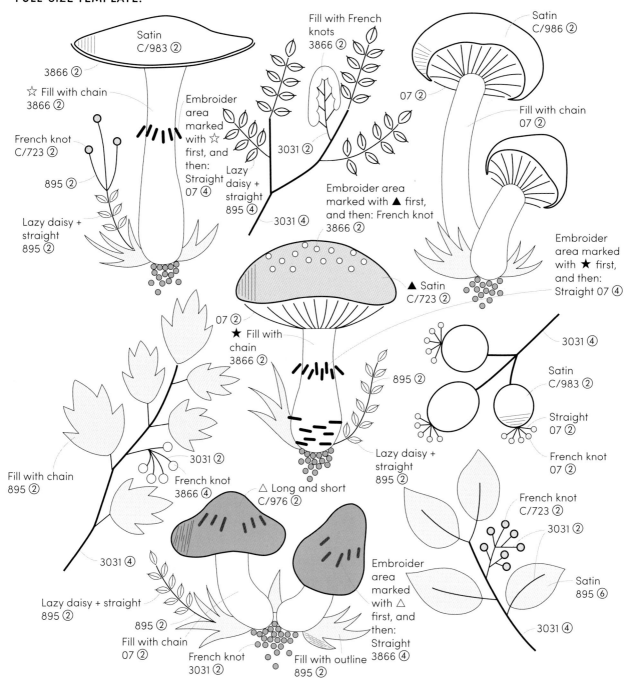

Satin C/983 ②

3866 ②

☆ Fill with chain 3866 ②

French knot C/723 ②

895 ②

Lazy daisy + straight 895 ②

Embroider area marked with ☆ first, and then: Straight 07 ④

Lazy daisy + straight 895 ④

Fill with French knots 3866 ②

3031 ②

3031 ④

Embroider area marked with ▲ first, and then: French knot 3866 ②

▲ Satin C/723 ②

07 ②

★ Fill with chain 3866 ②

895 ②

Satin C/986 ②

07 ②

Fill with chain 07 ②

Embroider area marked with ★ first, and then: Straight 07 ④

3031 ④

Satin C/983 ②

Straight 07 ②

French knot 07 ②

Lazy daisy + straight 895 ②

French knot C/723 ②

3031 ②

Satin 895 ⑥

3031 ④

Fill with chain 895 ②

3031 ④

Lazy daisy + straight 895 ②

895 ②

Fill with chain 07 ②

French knot 3031 ②

French knot 3866 ④

△ Long and short C/976 ②

Embroider area marked with △ first, and then: Straight 3866 ④

Fill with outline 895 ②

Christmas Rose Motif

SHOWN ON PAGE 38

MATERIALS:

- DMC Tapestry Wool (1 skein each): ECRU (unbleached white), 7327 (turquoise green), 7329 (moss green), 7426 (grass green), 7429 (dark green), 7510 (light gray), and 7583 (yellow green)
- DMC Six Strand Embroidery Floss (1 skein each): 500 (dark green) and 647 (light green)

NOTES:

- Use satin stitch unless otherwise noted. Use 1 strand unless otherwise noted.
- Areas worked in tapestry wool are noted with a T.
- Use six strand embroidery floss unless otherwise noted.

FULL-SIZE TEMPLATE:

Fill with French knots
T/7583 ①

Fill with chain
500 ③

T/7426

T/7510

T/ECRU

Long and short

T/7327

T/7329

T/7429

Outline
647 ⑥

Skiers Motif

SHOWN ON PAGE 37

MATERIALS:

- Appleton Crewel Wool (1 skein each): 296 (dark green), 356 (olive green), 749 (navy), and 834 (green)
- DMC Six Strand Embroidery Floss (1 skein each): 02 (light gray), 535 (gray), 543 (beige), 611 (sand beige), and 3021 (dark brown)

STITCH GUIDE (NOT A TEMPLATE):

- Use satin stitch unless otherwise noted.
- Areas worked in crewel wool are noted with a C.
- Use six strand embroidery floss unless otherwise noted.

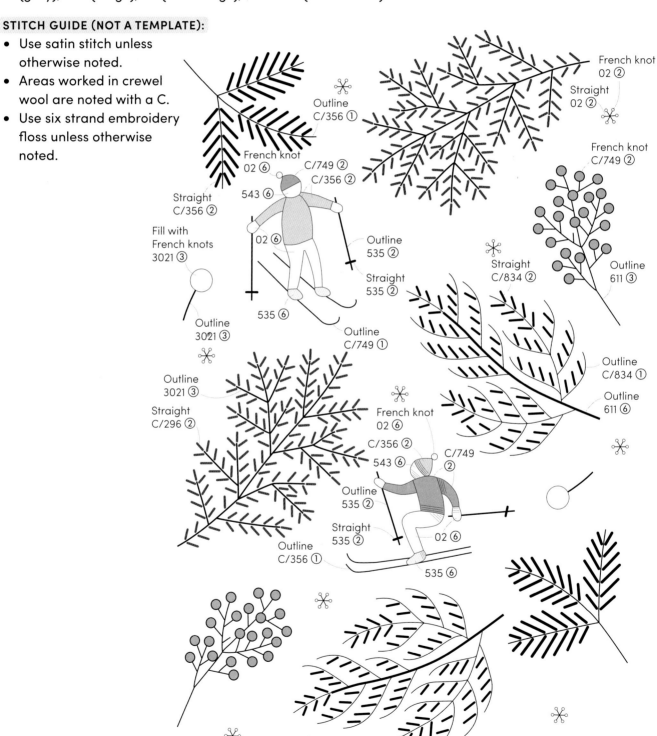

French knot
02 ②

Straight
02 ②

Outline
C/356 ①

French knot
C/749 ②

French knot
02 ⑥

C/749 ②
C/356 ②

543 ⑥

Straight
C/356 ②

Fill with
French knots
3021 ③

02 ⑥

Outline
535 ②

Straight
535 ②

Straight
C/834 ②

Outline
611 ③

535 ⑥

Outline
C/749 ①

Outline
3021 ③

Outline
C/834 ①

Outline
611 ⑥

Outline
3021 ③

Straight
C/296 ②

French knot
02 ⑥

C/356 ②

C/749
②

543 ⑥

Outline
535 ②

Straight
535 ②

02 ⑥

Outline
C/356 ①

535 ⑥

Christmas Square Botanical

SHOWN ON PAGE 39

MATERIALS:

- DMC Tapestry Wool (1 skein each): ECRU (unbleached white), 7379 (khaki), 7406 (light green), 7429 (dark green), 7519 (chestnut), 7540 (green), and 7583 (yellow green)
- DMC Six Strand Embroidery Floss (1 skein each): 505 (green), 610 (light brown), and 647 (light green)

NOTES:

- Use satin stitch unless otherwise noted. Use 1 strand unless otherwise noted.
- Areas worked in tapestry wool are noted with a T.
- Use six strand embroidery floss unless otherwise noted.

FULL-SIZE TEMPLATE:

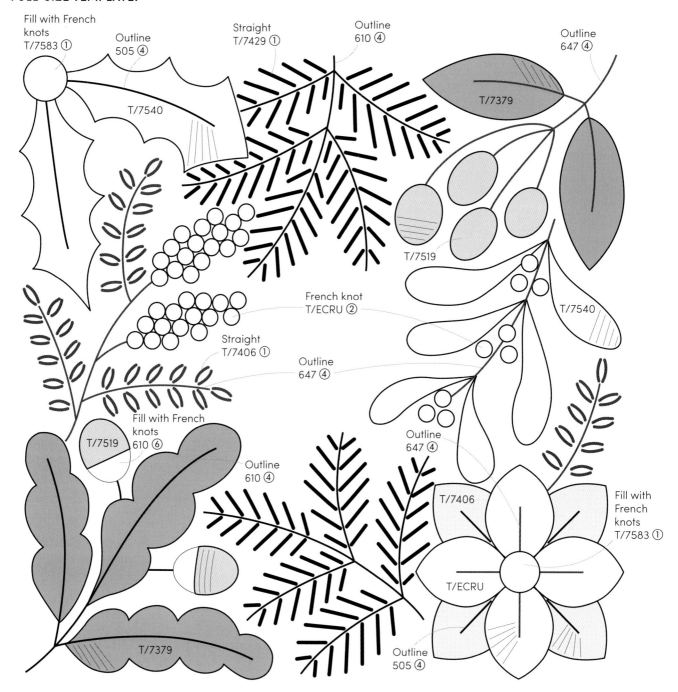

Embroidery Stitch Guide

Straight Stitch The appearance of this basic stitch changes based on the number of threads used. When worked in wool, this stitch has volume and is ideal for flowers and leaves.

Outline Stitch Use this stitch when embroidering long lines. Make sure to insert the needle and draw it out of the same hole in steps 1 and 3. Make many stitches along curves to produce a smooth line.

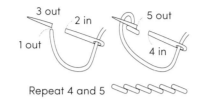

French Knot Stitch Wrap the thread around the needle, then insert the needle right next to the hole where the thread was drawn out of the fabric. Hold the wraps taut against the surface of the fabric as you pull the thread through.

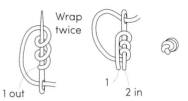

Chain Stitch Use this round stitch for embroidering lines and for filling small surfaces.

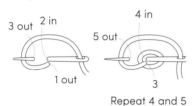

Lazy Daisy Stitch This stitch is commonly used to embroider petals.

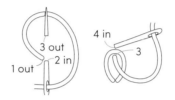

Lazy Daisy Stitch + Straight Stitch Work a straight stitch on top of a lazy daisy stitch to create voluminous shapes, such as leaves and fruits.

Satin Stitch Align several even straight stitches to fill a surface with satin stitch. This stitch is especially suitable when working with wool thread.

Long and Short Stitch Fill a surface by alternating long and short stitches. This stitch is mainly used for embroidering fan-shaped petals.

Backstitch This stitch is suitable for embroidering fine lines.

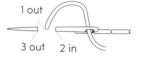

How to Stitch a Corner with Chain Stitch When you reach the corner, stop and change the angle of your stitching so it is perpendicular to the stitches you've already worked.

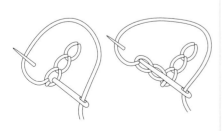

How to Fill a Surface with Chain Stitch or French Knots Work the outline of the design first, and then go back and fill the inside, following the shape of the outline as closely as possible. When filling a surface with chain stitch, take care not to leave gaps.

How to Stitch Flowers and Leaves with Long and Short Stitch or Satin Stitch Work stitches that radiate from the center and spread toward the left and right edges.

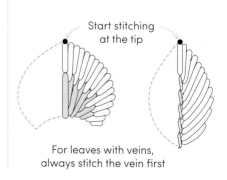

How to Make a Knot

Before you start stitching, you'll need to make a knot at the end of your thread. Thread the needle, and then wrap the end of the thread around the needle twice. Hold the wraps in place with your fingers as you pull the needle through. Move the knot to the end of the thread and tighten.

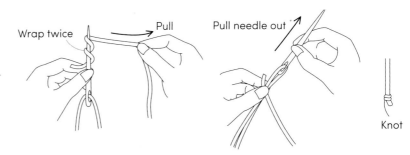

How to Start and Finish Stitching

When Stitching a Surface with Satin Stitch or Long and Short Stitch

Start: Insert your knotted thread through the fabric, making a few stitches inside the outline of the design in order to draw your needle out at the starting point. Embroider, covering these stitches as you work. Once you've made a few stitches, you can trim the knot. **Finish:** Bring the thread to the wrong side of the work. Insert the needle underneath a few stitches in both directions before trimming the excess thread.

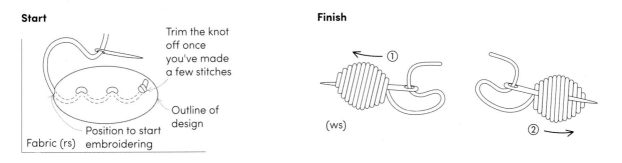

When Stitching Lines with Chain Stitch or Outline Stitch

Start: Insert your knotted thread through the fabric, making a few stitches along the outline of the design in order to draw your needle out at the starting point. Embroider, covering these stitches as you work. Once you've made a few stitches, you can trim the knot. **Finish:** Bring the thread to the wrong side of the work. Insert the needle underneath a few stitches before trimming the excess thread.

When Starting a New Thread in the Middle of the Work

If you're starting a new thread in the middle of the work, insert the knot through a few stitches on the wrong side, then draw the needle out at the starting point on the right side of the work. You can trim the knot off once you've made a few stitches.

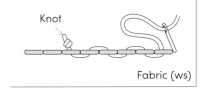